The Forest o

Ribchester, Hurst Green, Clitheroe, Downham and Whalley

by

JOHN DIXON

'The Roving Recusant'

HIGHER WHITEHALGH

With illustrations by
JANNA JÄRVINEN & JOHN DIXON

The Forest of Bowland
Ribchester, Hurst Green, Clitheroe, Downham and Whalley

By John Dixon

With illustrations by
Janna Järvinen & John Dixon

Published by Aussteiger Publications
Email: aussteiger_211@hotmail.com

Proof read and typeset by Sophie Dixon

Printed by
Lamberts Print & Design, Station Road, Settle,
North Yorkshire BD24 9AA

First Edition 2004

ISBN 1 872764 11 8

To the memory of Janna

Distributors: Lancashire Books, 213 Chorley Old Road,
Whittle-le-Woods, Chorley PR6 7NP. Tel. 01247-278613

Internet: www.lancsbooks.co.uk
The Historic Lancashire Organisation
'Promoting the Real Lancashire'

PLEASE OBSERVE THE COUNTRY CODE

AUSSTEIGER PUBLICATIONS

CONTENTS

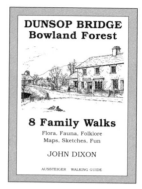

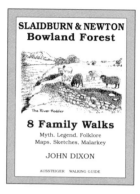

John Dixon is available for leading day, and weekend walks, throughout the year. John also lectures on the Bowland-Pennine region through organised field trips.

Contact Aussteiger for details and availability.

Information: www.lancsbooks.co.uk

Tel: 01200 443129   Aussteiger Publications

Email: aussteiger_211@hotmail.com

LANCASHIRE HISTORY QUARTERLY
www.hudson-history.co.uk

INTRODUCTION

Atecotti. The Oldest Ones.

'The Oldest Ones', were spoken of in hushed and whispered tones.
'The guardians of the Henges.' 'The readers of the stones.'
The ones who wore plumed feathers, and dwelt in tents of hide.
The ones who seemed to disappear like froth borne by the tide.
And mystery breeds legend, and saga finds a home.
For 'Atlantean' Atecotti, who threw back mighty Rome.
And story springs from story like the passing of the blood.
Fuelling tales of 'Hern the Hunter.', and Robin of the Hood.'
Though they were men of flesh, they lived as in a dream.
With a spirit, in each stone and tree; a God in every stream.
In harmony with fox, and bird, and earth, and star and bough.
The Atecotti reaped, and let sweet Nature push the plough.
An herbal lore and secret ways, that Druid masters knew.
The knowledge of 'The Oldest Ones', passed on to chosen few.
Not dead but living still they are, where wilderness is cherished.
Where men commune with Nature, Atecotti have not perished.
For still in ever 'fairy dell', on each stone circled, plain.
An Atecotti spirit dwells, and waits to come again.

DAVID HAZELL

The range and scope of this book take in some of my previous works, that are here extensively revised, with new source material and walking routes not covered in any other work – without doubt a great informative guide to walking and exploring the Ribble Valley.

Enjoy yourselves,

John Dixon, Clitheroe, 2004.

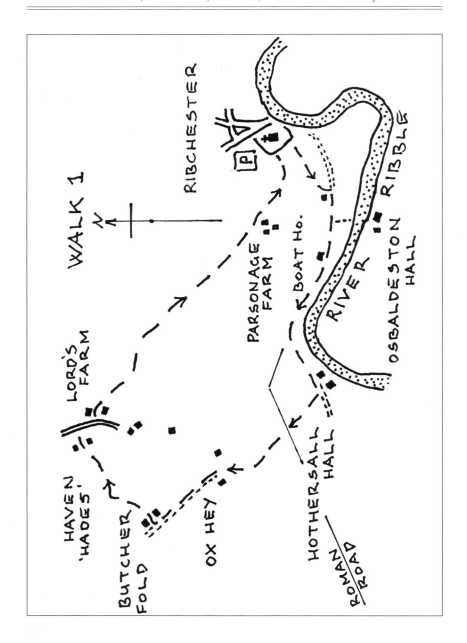

WALK 1

RIBCHESTER
GHOSTS, DEMONS & SEVERED HEADS

4¾ miles easy walking – riverside and field pasture

On this ramble we hear first of a bleeding ghost, then meet with the talkative spectre of an elderly cavalier. Later we shall come upon the trapped and petrified head of a demon whose story will unfold like a coil of rope. Finally, before crossing field and meadow on our return to Ribchester, we discover a friendly pair of Celtic stone heads with a gory tale to tell from our pre-Roman past.

VILLAGE CAR PARK TO VIEW OSBALDESTON HALL

Follow the road to the right to go through kissing-gate on left and on to the rear churchyard gate. Walk down the Roman ditch defences….

The slight ridge in front of the ditch is the line of the Roman fort rampart. In this area the western gate and corner tower have been located and excavated.

...and on to go over corner stile. Walk directly on to climb over hedge-stile and across the field then over a footbridge and through gate onto lane at Lower Barn Cottages. Follow the lane and go over hedge-stile on left. Walk to the river to view Osbaldeston Hall.

OSBALDESTON HALL

Upon the opposite bank of the Ribble stands the Elizabethan pile – once ancestral home of the Osbaldeston family, who first built a hall on the site in the 13th century. The small remains of a moat from the early period can still be discerned in the grounds today. The Osbaldestons played a major role in those events that shaped English history. Their number fought at Agincourt and Flodden Field and were prominent during the Civil Wars, only to have their line come to an end with the death of Alexander Osbaldeston in 1752.

The most recalled member of that family today is one Thomas Osbaldeston who slew his sister's husband in a duel in a room at the Hall in 1606. Even afterwards, the floorboards were ineradicably stained with the blood of his victim, Edward Walsh a member of the Southworth family of Samlesbury, whose restless spirit periodically returns to this room, moaning and gliding with arms uplifted to expose blood pouring from a gash in his chest.

OSBALDESTON HALL

Thomas's initials are recorded on a doorhead at the rear of the Hall dated 1593.

There was formerly a Roman figure of Hercules built into a wall of the house, depicting him holding a club in his right hand with the

Height, 2 feet 6 inches.

skin of the Numaean lion thrown over his left shoulder. Other fragments of Roman masonry have been located built into the fabric of the building.

The heron in flight is a familiar sight on the Ribble today, yet near the banks it stands unnoticed like a wizened grey post with black eye-stripes. If you watch closely you will see the bird unfurl its neck and start to stalk fish.

During the month of June sea trout start their movements upriver to the spawning grounds. This journey is indicated by the presence of the coastal cormorant and the red-breasted merganser duck, the former being most often sighted on this Ribchester reach of the Ribble.

The Ribchester Ferry, which ran across the river here, is first mentioned in 1335 when Adam Bibby of Ribchester granted William de Bradley the right to carry people across the Ribble. Northbound travellers would swing a lantern in the evening to attract the attention of the boatman at Boathouse Farm. The wood behind the ferry point at Osbaldeston became known as Flashers Wood. Today Boathouse Farm is a number of dwellings, the old roadside cottage reminding us of a bygone age.

RIBCHESTER BOAT TO HOTHERSALL HALL

Return to the lane and continue on, passing the former boatman's house, to the bottom of the hill rise via gateways and stiles. Walk up the rise to view the line of the Roman road.

The stones are said to mark the line of the Roman road that once ran between Preston and the fort at Ribchester – part of a trans-Pennine route used to control the Brigantian tribes.

It is along this riverbank path that there have been many sightings and nocturnal meetings with a shadowy elderly gent attired in the costume of a cavalier. The ghost offers a friendly greeting and goes on to inquire on how things are going locally these days. The spectre refers to himself as 'Mr Walker of Alston'. Apparently, the Ribchester Parish Register records that on January 16th 1735, William Walker of Alston, a Cavalier, was buried aged 122 – probably the oldest Lancastrian.

Walk to the left, and down to pass over stile by gate. Walk on to view Hothersall Hall.

HOTHERSALL HALL

HOTHERSHALL HALL

The splendid hall we see today was built by the Bury woollen manufacturer Jonathan Openshaw in 1856, on the site of an older hall. No part of the former house remains, with the exception of a carved stone built into the wall of one of the outbuildings on which are the arms of Hothersall together with the initials of Thomas Hothersall and the date 1695.

For his part in the Jacobite Rising of 1715, Thomas Hothersall along with Thomas Shuttleworth of Alston Old Hall, were executed. Being an Outlaw and Roman Catholic, Thomas forfeited the family estate of Hothersall.

From the time of the Catholic persecutions of Henry the Eight, up to the Rebellion of 1715, Mass was celebrated in secret at Hothersall Hall, Osbaldeston Hall and several other houses in the district.

HOTHERSALL HALL TO HAVEN

Follow the lane up to find a stone head wedged in the boughs of a tree at the farm drive.

In the fork of a tree on the lane above the hall can be found a horrific and grotesque stone head. This was dug up by a farmer at Hothersall and placed in its present position. To Lancashire Jacobites it represents the executed head of the outlaw Thomas Hothersall; others say that the head is that of the petrified Hothersall Boggart. Legend hereabouts informs us that a demon from Hades had undertaken to oblige a local farmer with three wishes for the surrender of his soul.

The farmer's first two wishes were for wealth and good fortune, but his third was a crafty move to avoid damnation. He wished the boggart to spin a rope from the sands of the Ribble and in the event of failure he must consent to be laid under a laurel tree there to turn into stone (for a demon cannot rot, only fuse into granite etc).

Each time the boggart spun a rope the farmer poured water over it and the rope disintegrated. Eventually he gave up his efforts and accepted his fate, whereby the farmer escaped the demon's clutches and saved his soul. Boggarts haunt many spots around Ribchester so be careful of talking to strangers on the Eve of the Moon.

Go through a gate on the right and walk up the track into the big field. Walk up the field to go through a hedge gateway. Walk directly on and through a gate. Follow track to Ox Hey lane. Left, walk along the lane to Butcher Fold.

Butcher Fold is so called because one of the buildings here was once the local slaughterhouse.

Enter the farmyard and walk through to leave by field-gate. Follow the farm track on to enter field via gate. Walk on and over fence-stile. Then over to the right to enter wood via stile. The track leads us down to go over stile on the left. Walk up to Haven.

THE HAVEN STONE HEADS

HADES FARM

Set into the gable of the porch at Haven (formerly Hades Farm) are two Celtic stone heads. They were once set into a low wall opposite the house.

The survival of the true Celtic stone heads is linked to the ancient cult of the severed head. To the Celts, in the head rested everything that made men what they are – it was the seat of the Celtic equivalent of the soul. Celtic warriors were head-hunters who kept the heads of their foe as trophies and Brigantian forts were adorned with human heads. Stone heads appear to have represented Celtic deities such as Maponus the northern god. Stone heads have been invested with special properties by local superstition, right up to the present day. Relics of an older paganism survive in many forms of modern Christianity: green men, imps, bearded ogres and whores adorn many of our local churches. The power of pagan superstition is long-lived and not easily set aside by reason.

HAVEN TO RIBCHESTER

Follow lane to road. Turn right and walk along the road to go left along Lord's Farm drive. The farm lane leads us past Kays Barn and Lord's Farm, on down past a barn, to two iron gates. Go through LH gate and walk on to go over stile by gate. Follow line of LH boundary……

I saw a good few deer here bolting from the thorn & holly hedge.

…to enter an old track behind the hedge via stile. Carry on to pass over fence-stile. Walk on…

Here at Three Turns there once stood the Dutton Gibbet. This was a triangular frame supported on three posts on which the bodies of executed criminals were left hanging as a warning and deterrent to others. The most noted to swing from here was the highwayman Ned King.

Left at junction and walk on to cross the road at First Farm Lane on the right. Follow farm lane on, passing Grindlestone House and on some way to go over fence-stile on left. Walk down the wooded ravine to cross footbridge on up to go over fence-stile. Cross the field then over footbridge and on across the next field to meet Bailey Hall Lane. Left and walk along the lane to Titum House.

Titum House commands an agreeable prospect above Bailey Brook. Built in the Jacobean style it should mature well over the coming years. As to the name, could it be Latin?

For many years now people have reported sightings of a heavily clad Roman soldier just standing and looking from the trees beyond the house. The apparition is said to be very clear at first but soon fades to a mere shade. One gentleman gave me a very good description of the ghostly warrior. He wore scale armour beneath a fur cloak and heavy gaiters covering his lower legs. On his head was a conical helmet, with a vertical metal frame. A sword hung on his right side. This attire was characteristic of a Sarmatian heavy cavalryman.

The Sarmatians, an Iranian speaking people who came from east of the Carpathians, had a large veteran settlement in the Ribble Valley based at Whalley and an active service heavy cavalry unit stationed at Ribchester.

After the withdrawal of the Roman army from Britain in the opening years of the 5th century, the Sarmatians, who had been stationed here in the North since 175 AD, continued to live on their accustomed sites as a warrior elite of armoured horsemen.

The territorial divisions of pre-Conquest Lancashire are easily explained when one looks at such a society based on cavalry units.

Aussteiger is soon to publish a major work on the origins of Lancashire, that will revolutionize current academic thinking. Perhaps this is what the old spectral warrior has been waiting for – a valid account of the heritage his people and our ancestry laid down in 'The Age of Arthur'.

Continue along the lane to Longridge Road and the Punch Bowl.

THE STORY OF NED KING

At the turn of the 18th century many things were afoot in Lancashire. The stirrings of industrialisation could be felt throughout the county. Men of enterprise and greed were quickly forming a new class and social structure based on the exploitation of labour, capital and resources, without a care for tradition and practice. This led to much resentment and bad feeling towards this new ethic. Predestination was to prevail over free will and choice, the age of the Antichrist was in the ascendant.

Delinquency and recusancy are hallmarks of the true and honest Lancastrian in the face of evil and oppression and this can be manifest in many ways and deeds, in brotherhood or as sole agent.

One such bold and solitary insurgent was William Edward Bell of Dutton. William dwelt in a secluded moorland cottage on the southern flank of Jeffrey Hill and was known to local folk as 'Wild Ned o' th' Fell', due to his singular mind and countenance.

Many generations of rebel blood pumped through his veins, untamed thoughts of insurrection and retribution haunted his waking hours and in his dreams past glories rallied forth and held sway.

At first Ned tried to drum up support to redress the situation he foresaw, but the Palatine was in no mood with so many men away in foreign wars and emancipation being held as the carrot to wage slavery. Ned was a man out of time and out of step with the new age. Such a man will follow his own path and make his own destiny regardless of consequence or consideration.

Ned took on the role of a freebooter and set forth on a terrible lawless adventure that was to wreak havoc along the King's highway between Wigan and Lancaster.

From his hillside redoubt Ned would study ship disembarkation times and coaching tables and would pick out likely travellers worthy of plucking. When sure of his information he would sally forth on his trusty stead Black Tarquin, pistols and sword at hand, with not a care or thought for others loss or forfeit of life or limb.

Such was the luck and measure of his deeds that he became the terror of every turnpike with yarns of his infamy being recounted in every roadside tavern and inn.

One inn in which men kept a firm hold of their tongues was the Punch Bowl Inn at Bailey Green. For this was the watering hole of Ned's fancy.

As Ned's outrages and notoriety spread, so did the net of King's Justice trawl wide in search of the old receiver, 'King of the High Toby.'

Eventually the net closed in and his luck ran out. The King's troopers had run him down and surrounded the Punch Bowl and with fixed bayonets began a room to room search of the buildings there. On entering the hay barn where Ned was hold-up, a fire-flight ensued and four troopers fell to Ned's volly. Reloading two brace of pistols Ned mounted the steps to the inn's gallery for his final stand. Flint hit steel and powder flared and a hail of lead forced Ned to cower for cover in the right-hand corner of the gallery. Holed through in six places, but still alive, Ned was overpowered, dragged down and chained. There would be no trial for Ned. He was ignomiously horse-pulled to the old gibbet that stood at Three Turns at the top of Gallows Lane some three-quarter mile west. There the blooded remains of Ned body hung as an example for all to see and for many weeks after did birds' feast of the carrion.

So ended the life of William Edward Bell, but not the times – his ghost haunts the place to this day. Moanings have been heard among the rafters. There are unexplained noises along the corridors at dead of night and bottles unaccountably fall from selves. And on the night before the full moon the fall of Black Tarquin's hoofs can be heard in a spectral gallop along the Longridge Road urged on with shouts from its phantom rider.

The Punch Bowl Inn, built in 1793, reputedly suffered so much inconvenience from highwayman Ned's ghost for a hundred years and more, that in 1942 a priest from Stoneyhurst College performed a Rite of Exorcism.

Since that time reports of Ned's errant spirit being aboard have been few, but such a fellow and tales of his deeds are difficult to lay down. And as new murmurings of discontent once again begin to surface in a troubled realm, do not be surprised if his apparition became manifest once more.

THE PUNCH BOWL

The Punch Bowl inn at Bailey Green stands on the Longridge to Clitheroe road opposite Bailey House. The frontage and rear gardens are always well maintained, reflecting over 200 years standing. A datestone, set into the watershot stone frontage, records the date 1793 with the initials R. C. E.. Inside is a fine restaurant catering for those wanting anything from a bar snack, right through to evening dinner. The beer is Thwaites – the best in Lancashire.

PUNCH BOWL TO BAILEY HOUSE

Pass the pub to go up first farm lane on left to Bailey House.

BAILEY HOUSE

This 17th century farmhouse displays many fine mullioned windows with slender hood moulding above the ground floor and gable windows. The west

BAILEY HOUSE

gable is a very good example of watershot stonework, now a lost tradition. How great it would be to see this technique introduced once more. So much better than the rough stone cladding, so wrong and awful, that so-called 'stone masons' throw up today.

BAILEY HOUSE TO HURST GREEN

Pass through gates by side of barn and follow track to big field. Walk up to the LH side of Doe Hill to go around the hill to the Trig Point.

Wonderful views – a lovely spot this.

Walk on to go over fence-stile at New House onto lane. Right and walk down the road to junction. Left and walk on to enter Cut Thorn yard on left. Pass through gate on left and walk round to the right to go over stile by gate. Walk to the left and then pass over fence-stile. Walk over the field and over fence-stile in corner and on down to cross footbridge.

What a lovely spot here by the old converted mill.

Walk up the drive to pass through gate. Left and walk on by the side of the fancy garage to meet lane. Walk up to Hurst Green.

> Of all the trees in England,
> Oak, Elder, Elm, and Thorn,
> The Yew alone burns lamps of peace
> For them that lie forlorn.
> *Walter de la Mare.*

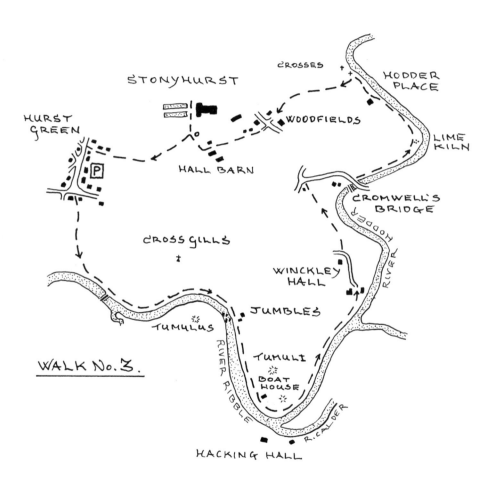

WALK 3

STONYHURST
TOLKIEN'S SHIRE

5½ miles – riverside and fields paths – easy walking
Car Parking at the Village Hall, Hurst Green – donation box

To wander through the Forest of Days, whose floor is carpeted with the countless foliage of the Tree of Tales, is the true joy of lovers of language and literature in all its forms and origins.

J. R. R. Tolkien was such a roamer in that enchanted place from where he laboured to collect a few fallen leaves, many torn and decayed, others fresh off the bough, each a unique embodiment of a pattern that formed in his mind and imagination a fantasy tale from a pre-Arthurian past.

'The Lords of the Rings' was the culmination of his wanderings. But it was more than an imaginary world. Middle-earth contains many things besides elves and fays and besides dwarfs, witches, trolls, giants or dragons: it holds the seas, the sun, the moon, the sky; and the earth and all things that are in it: tree and bird, water and stone, wine and bread and ourselves, mortal men when we are enchanted.

The 'Master of Middle-earth' wrote much of his trilogy during his stays at Stoneyhurst College. I like to think that he knew this walk, as it is one intended to inspire and delight.

HURST GREEN TO HACKING BOAT

There are public toilets by St. Peters Club – both good watering holes.

Walk down through the yard on the left of the Shireburn Arms to go over a stile by gate. Walk down by the hedge and ditch to cross a stream and on down a rise between two streams to go over stile and footbridge. Walk on, down to the riverbank

JUMBLES

via stiles and footbridge. Follow the riverside path to Jumbles.

Once a farm, Jumbles is now two dwelling houses. The main house is built in the late Stewart style. A dated tablet to the side of the front door informs us that the house was built by John Hill and Richard, his son in 1723. In the garden stands the weight from an old cheese press.

The house takes its name from Jumbles Rocks, an ancient and hazardous fording point on the river that links the two Bronze Age sites of Winckley Lowes and Brockhall Eases.

JUMBLES

On your way to Jumbles you may have noticed a stone cross squatting on the summit of the sharp hill south-east of Hurst Green. This is the Delph or Gills Cross, an ancient pedestal surmounted by an ornate 19th century cross shaft. The cross originally stood by the main road above Cross Gills Farm and was then known as Cross Kells.

Continue on to the former Boat House.

HACKING BOAT

CROSS GILLS, HURST GREEN

The recently restored Boat House is s reminder of the days when a ferry transported travellers and wanderers alike across the waters between Winckley, Hacking and Little Mytton. Some years ago the old boat was found in a nearby field barn (now gone) and was taken away to be restored. It is now on display in Clitheroe Castle Museum (for which a large fee is charged for entry – scandalous, given that it is owned by the public).

THE BOAT HOUSE, WINKLEY LOWES

In times past a bell was mounted upon a pole on the Hacking bank of the river. This acted as a signal to the ferryman requesting his or her – the last ferryman was a woman – services.

THE WINVKLEY LOWES

Two large mounds stand near to the Boat House, both of which are man-made. The one to the west was excavated by Rev. J. R. Luck of Stoneyhurst College in 1894. The tumulus revealed a cinerary urn of c.1250 BC, which contained the cremated remains of a body. Also found were a young man's skull and a flint knife, a boy's skull and a child's skull.

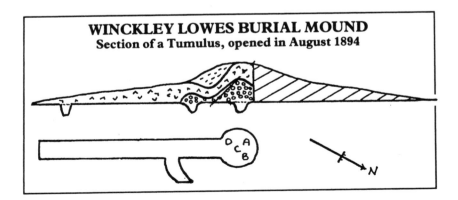

WINCKLEY LOWES BURIAL MOUND
Section of a Tumulus, opened in August 1894

The burial is one of a important person – probably a local chieftain – buried near the ancient natural ford at Jumbles which must have been well known and used by man even in Neolithic times.

The eastern mound is known as Loe Hill and has only recently been declared man-made. No major excavation work has been carried out on the mound and its purpose remains uncertain.

Some suppose that it was built after the Battle of Billington in 798 AD; towards the close of the 8th century the Anglo-British kingdom of Northumbria was fraught with internal conflict.

In 774 the Northumbrians drove their King, Alhred from York and took Aethelred, son of Moll to be their lord. Arthelred reigned for four years, being driven from his kingdom in the revolt of 778 which was led by Aethelbald and Heardberht, who instated Aelfwald as their lord. The year 789 was the downfall and death of Aelfwald who was slain by Sicga.

(Professor Tolkien, an Anglo-Saxon scholar, would have been aware and loved all this.)

His nephew, Osred son of Alhred succeeded to the kingdom. The following year Osred was betrayed and driven out of Northumbria and Aethelred returned again to his kingdom. In 794 Aethelred was killed by his own court and after many months of anarchy and savage Viking raids, Eardwulf succeeded to the perilous and unstable dignity of the Northumbrian Crown.

In 798 a rival faction had gathered strength and was prepared to contest the government of the kingdom with Eardwulf. The decisive battle between the king and the would-be usurpers took place hereabouts in the same year. The chiefs of this conspiracy were Wada and Alric, son of Heardberht, both implicated in the former rebellion which ended in the deposition and death of the previous king Aethelred. Simeon of Durham gives us an account of the battle:

"A confederacy was made of the murderers of King Aethelred; Wada, chief in that conspiracy, with his force went against Eardwulf, in a place called by the English Billangahoh (Billington), near Walalege (Whalley), and on either side many were slain; Wada, the chief, with his men, was put to flight, and King Eardwulf regally achieved victory over his enemies."

The Anglo-Saxon Chronicle for that year states:

In this year in Spring, on 2nd April, there was a great battle at Whalley in Northumbria, and there was slain Alric, son of Heardberht, and many others with him."

The importance of Whalley cannot to understated in pre-Conquest times and is a major key to the understanding of the period from the end of the Roman occupation to the Domesday Survey.

A third mound once stood across the Ribble at Brockhall Eases. During the summer of 1836 Thomas Hubbersty, the farmer at Brockhall, was removing a large mound of earth when he discovered a stone-lined cist. This was said to contain human bones and the rusty remains of some iron spearheads. The whole crumbled to dust on exposure to air, one is tempted to describe it as a 1st millennium BC burial.

Stone-lined cists are known in the Iron Age but these are invariably surface graves. Barrow inhumations of this type have been found in Scotland, though such mounds are cairns and not mounds of earth. Again, whilst primary inhumations in barrows are not uncommon in the post-Roman period, stone-lined cists are very rare. Only one site, Chelmorton in Derbyshire, has been recorded in the north of England.

It is also possible to see the mound as a Bronze Age earthen bowl-barrow; consequently, one could put the barrow into the wider pattern of Bronze Age settlement in the area. Its close proximity to Winckley Lowes might indicate that the site had some ritual or territorial significance. Given the lack of dateable remains the site must remain the subject of speculation.

HACKING HALL

On the opposite bank of the river stands the magnificent Jacobean mansion of Hacking Hall, resplendent with its many mullioned gabled frontage. The hall was built by Thomas Livesey of Livesey, father of Sir Thomas Walmeley's mother, in 1607 and later added to by Sir Thomas, a noted circuit judge.

There are some good family tales here, but that is for another book of Ribble Valley walks.

A superbly designed Y-span footbridge is due to be erected at Hacking Boat to link Hacking with Little Mytton and Winckley. This will be great for walks and give a well-needed boost to tourism in the Ribble Valley. I think that J. R. R. Tolkien would have approved of the wonderful contemporary concept.

Winckley Hall

HACKING BOAT TO STONYHURST COLLEGE

Follow the path and track by the Hodder to enter Winckley Hall farmyard.

Winckley Hall was part of the Knights Hospitalliers estate in Aighton and Bailey which was treated as part of their manor at Stydd. The old hall, now a farm displays little of it ancient past.

The central section is the oldest part of the house and to the rear are two splendid mullioned and transomed windows with hood mouldings above. Also at the rear is a 'Donkey Walk' or 'Horse-gin,' complete with its old grinding stones. This was used for grinding grain up till the late 19th century.

The most notable occupant was one Dorothy Winckley who through marriage moved to Pleasington Hall, near Blackburn. She married first a Southworth, then a Hoghton and finally Thomas Ainsworth. It is claimed that she is the 'White Lady' who wanders the lanes around the Great Hall at Samlesbury (see Brigantia, Vol.11).

An ancient cross once stood in the grounds of Winckley Hall in an elevated position at the top of Spring Wood overlooking the Hodder. In 1929 the entire cross including the pedestal and plinth, was removed and it now stands as a headstone of a grave in Great Mitton churchyard – a memorial to Hartley Baldwin of New Winkley Hall. Such arrogance – the plinth and pedestal should be returned to their historical context.

The place-name 'Winckley' is of Celtic (British) origin – vindo (white), kaito (wood), in old Welsh - gwyn coed, meaning 'the glade in the white wood.'

Upon leaving the farmyard, notice the duck ponds. These are the remains of a moat that once surrounded the old hall on all sides.

Walk up the drive to go through kissing-gate on right beyond New Winckley Hall.

Notice the old pigsty over on the left.

Cross the field directly, over stile and across the field to follow fenceline, down and over stiles onto the Road.

A lovely view walking down from here of the 'Lion of Pendle' and Worsa Hill.

Walk down to the Lower Hodder Bridge.

Standing slightly down river is the remains of the old Hodder Bridge, known locally as C r o m w e l l ' s Bridge. Oliver Cromwell and his army crossed this bridge and ford on the eve of the Battle of Preston in 1648. Cromwell stayed the night at Stoneyhurst after a forced march from Knaresborough with 8,500 men who encamped within the deer park.

The bridge was built by Sir Richard Shireburn in 1562 at a cost of £70. In 1569 a collection was made in the Blackburn Hundred towards further building work on the bridge.

Across the bridge on the Mitton Magna side, stands an old milestone of 1766 erected by John Shireburn. 'To Lanca*f*ter 16M. To Whalley M3. I:S 1766'.

(Old English '*f*' was 's'. 'Y' was sounded as 'th' hence 'ye' was always pronounced 'the'. Complicated thing when reading old manuscripts.)

Many strange objects adorn the farmsteads of the Lower Hodder. Two stone heads and an old font of 1710 are but a few. The recordings and drawings here are from a study by the late Mrs Alice Smith of Copster Green. Alice was a great wanderer and a joy to have known.

One head is finely carved from sandstone, showing a male with long flowing hair and a fine beard. Around the neck he wears a ruff.

The other is very grand showing classical influences. The headgear seems Eastern or mediaeval, the beard and moustache long and flowing. This head was found on the south side of Jeffrey Hill near to the Roman road.

Walk back to the Stoneyhurst side of the bridge and follow the riverside lane...

Kemple End, the wooded end of Longridge Fell, comes into view as we come to the grassy mound of an old lime kiln. Look out for herons on the river.

...to the turreted buildings of Hodder Place, via three kissing-gates.

This impressive building of 1780 was used as a Novitiate and later as a preparatory school. It is now divided into apartments and is privately owned.

Walk down the track to cross a castellated bridge.

Here stands the plinth and pedestal of a former cross memorial to a student at Stoneyhurst College for the priesthood , who was drowned in the Hodder on the 5th May 1877 when 25 years of age.

Another cross stands high above the river on steeply-shelving ground and is also a memorial to a Stonyhurst student for the priesthood who was drowned on July 31 1857 in his 26th year.

Wild garlic, wood anemones, lesser celandine and bluebells carpet the floor here beneath the thin Spring canopy – a lovely time to visit.

Follow the path upstream to go over a footbridge and up many steps...

Did you get to the top without a rest?

...to walk above the wooded glen and pass over a fence stile. Follow line of fence/hedge to go over ladder-stile by gate. The lane leads us to Woodfields and New Lodge.

Woodfields is a converted 17th century house which is now dated 1813, with the initials N. C. A. Four cottages across the way also carry these initials with the date of 1810.

WOODFIELDS

The earlier parts of the house can be seen on the side, once the original frontage. Two mullioned windows and a string mould attest to its early foundation. Inside is a richly decorated fire surround bearing the initials A. H. Built into the corner of an outbuilding is half the base of an old cheese press.

Tolkien's son Michael lived at Woodfields and planted a copse to his father's memory following his death in 1973. J. R.R. Tolkien stayed at nearby New Lodge on his visits to Stoneyhurst.

Walk to the road and cross into Hall Barn Farm Lane. Walk on...

Good views of Pendle, Whalley Nab and Billington Moor and soon the cupola crowned turrets of Stoneyhurst come into vision.

...to pass by the rear of the barn to a lane.

Though stone is the predominant material, inside the Hall Great Barn five enormous oak cruck trusses dominate the pile. These date to the 15th century and illustrate just how fine the oak once was.

The garden pavilions are very elegant with their concave-sided pyramid roofs and narrow Queen Anne windows. The keystone of the doorways is a Chinaman's face.

Walk up to the Observatory and continue on to view the church and the front of the college.

STONEYHURST COLLEGE

The most prominent house in the Ribble Valley is without doubt that of Stoneyhurst. It was the main residence of the Shireburn family until 1794 when it was placed at the disposal of the Jesuit Fathers of Liege. Today it is a Roman Catholic boarding school.

The Building we see today was started by Hugh Shireburn in c.1523, the major part being the work of Sir Richard Shireburn who began work with the gatehouse in 1592. Additions and alterations, especially in the gardens where made by Sir Nicholas Shireburn who inherited in 1690. His daughter and heir, the Duchess of Norfolk made a few alterations, one of which was to bring the Bailey Chapel east window to be incorporated into the main frontage.

During the Civil wars, General Oliver Cromwell stayed overnight at Stoneyhurst and is said to have slept upon the table, now known as 'Oliver Cromwell's Table,' with pistol and sword at his side. It was thought that he was only too wary of assassination, for the Shireburns were well known Papists. Early the following morning he marched his army the length of Longridge Fell to meet the Scottish Army under James, Duke of Hamilton. They met north of Preston on Ribbleton Moor. The encounter is known to history as the Battle of Preston, though the last action was actually fought on Warrington Bridge.

TO HURST GREEN

Return to the Observatory corner to go through an iron field-gate. Walk along by the lower fence, down and up to go through three kissing-gates. On by the walled gardened cottages on Smithy Row, into the village.

The Post Office and Village Store is also a Café and is well recommended as are St. Peters Club and The Eagle and Child.

> Learn now the lore of Living Creatures
> First name the four, the free peoples:
> Eldest of all, the elf-children;
> Dwarf the delver, dark are his houses;
> Ent the earthborn, old as mountains;
> Man the mortal, master of horses.
>
> *Treebeard.*

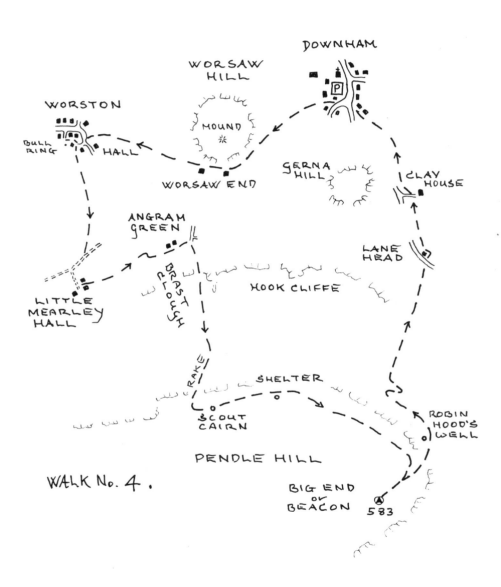

WALK No. 4.

WALK 4

DOWNHAM
MAJESTIC PENDLE

8 miles, one stiff climb from Angram Green to the Scout cairn, then the rest is pure joy. Parking and toilets at Downham.

This walk is designed to give you a long look at the great bulk of Pendle from the valley floor. Don't be put of by the steep rise – 'slowly, slowly catch the monkey' – it is easier than it looks, the ridge walk to the summit and the decent to Downham are superb. The initial wander through Worston and Mearley is leisurely, rewarding and it gets the old body going. Lots to see and lots of do, so off we go.

DOWNHAM CAR PARK TO WORSTON

Leave the car park to go up the 1st drive on the right and pass through stile by gate. Walk directly on to go through gate. Follow line of RH fence,...

Now the whole Lion Back of Pendle comes into vision.

...through squeeze-stile and on to end of wall. Veer to the left and cross the fields to go through kissing-gates. The path leads us under Worsaw Hill to go through gate at Worsaw End Farm.

The film 'Whistle Down The Wind,' staring Alan Bates and Hayley Mills was shot on location in Downham Village and at Worsaw End in 1961. Many locals were used as extras, as is the case with the TV comedy 'Born and Bred' also shot in Downham.

Pass over stile by gate on right and walk directly on to go through kissing-gate. Continue on over the field to go through kissing-gate into field lane. Left and walk on into Worston via

gate. The Calf's Head is to the right.

WORSTON

I found the Calf's Head a great pub for a mid-day stop. The food and service was excellent and the beer hit the spot. Room layout is spacious and the lovely garden provided a magnificent bonus. I shall return again soon.

Worston's claim in local 'witchlore' is that the Black Arts may have been in play here. Opposite the pub stands Crow Hill Cottage, an old building with origins in the 1500's. Some years ago, when a fireplace was being altered, clay effigies into which pins had been stuck were discovered. The old pagan ways still hold in many parts of Lancashire and old belief in the White Goddess is hard to displace. A small circular window of the house is known to locals as the 'Witches Window' and figures in many local tales.

> I am a wide flood on a plain,
> I am a wind on the deep waters,
> I am a hawk on a cliff,
> I am a hill of poetry.
> Pendle.

Walk past the pub's car park to go left by houses and over a footbridge. The path leads upstream...

This was once a very untidy footpath and credit must go to those who have tided it up and keep it well maintained. The large stone with its iron ring is now clear for all to see.

This was the local place for bull-baiting, cock-fighting and wrestling matches in former times. Now television and computers are the bait.

BULL-BAITING RING
WORSTON

...to the bridge and Worston Hall.

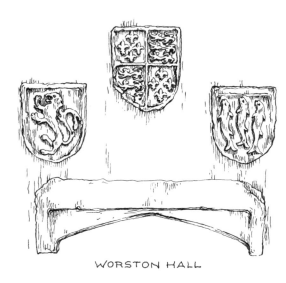

WORSTON HALL

The porch displays three heraldic shields. The first bears a lion rampant, the arms of Percy; the second is quarterly France and England; the third has on it three lucies or pikes, the arms of Lacy. Along with a large doorhead built into the garden wall and a Tudor doorhead above a garden doorway are all that remain of the Old Worston Hall of Richard Greenacres, built in 1577 from the stones of Sawley or Whalley Abbey.

The Greenacres were a powerful family around Clitheroe after the Reformation, being related to the Receiver General for Lancashire, they acquired much land on 'the nod,' became MP's and governors of Clitheroe Grammar

Worston Hall

School. Being well in with an estate agent has its perks.

WORSTON TO LITTLE MEARLEY HALL

Walk back across the bridge, right, and then left around the building to go over stile by gate. Walk up the field to go over

fence stile and on to go through small iron gate. Follow line of fence up to farm lane. Right and walk along to go up Little Mearley Hall drive.

LITTLE MEARLEY HALL

The farm dogs joyfully yelp at our arrival at this most rustic of true working farms in the Valley – and long may it remain so. (The dogs gave JK, a 'writer of copy,' the 'bum's rush' when he came by this way – and rightly so.)

One cannot fail to marvel at the splendour of the early 16th century bay window that came from the Abbot's House of Sawley or Whalley Abbey after the Dissolution, gift of the Receiver General for Lancashire.

The rear of the hall is late 16th century at its best. A stone tablet above the large Tudor doorway bears the arms of Nowell quartered with those of Walmsley and a date 1590, with the initials C. N. & E. N.: Christopher Nowell who married Elizabeth, daughter of Thomas Walmsley of Cold Cotes.

Other carved Abbey fragments are to be found here. But as always, please ask the farmer or his wife before making a close inspection of the Hall – if not too busy you will find them very friendly and accommodating.

LITTLE MEARLEY HALL

LITTLE MEARLEY TO PENDLE BIG END

Walk up the farm drive to pass through farm buildings on the left via three small gates. Go through the field gate...

Often a friendly Shetland pony is mooching around here.

...and follow line of wall to enter field via gate. Walk directly on, then down to the left a little to go through small gate at tall trees. Walk on by RH fence to go through gate on right and walk up to go through next gate. Walk on by LH fence...

Over to the left we gain a fine view of Worsaw Hill. Notice the little mound on the summit. This unexcavated bowl barrow testifies to settlement at Worston in pre-Roman times.

The Roman road passes very close to the village and during road works in 1778 a large coin horde was discovered. Some Roman nobleman (or Romano-British reeve) had deposited 1,000 silver denarii of the Higher Early Empire and a bronze lamp within an earthenware urn. The nine workmen who found the horde divided the coins amongst themselves, but about 350 were recovered and given to the ladies of the manor and a Mr Robinson. The earliest of the coins were those of Augustus.

...to cross Burst Clough Brook at Angram Green.

Angram Green is dated 1879 TPH, but some parts of the house are older: notice the 17th century mullioned windows on the north face of the farmhouse.

Burst or Brast Clough is the deep gully above us. But what of the name?

Well, imagine if you will Pendle as a giant cistern with a gritstone lid, beneath which are sandstones and shales 'floating' atop of a great volume of water contained within a limestone tank. When fissures occur in the tank walls the pressure of water can cause a fracture to allow water to burst forth.

Such an event took place at the time of the Dissolution and again in 1669 at a time of Dissention, especially in Lancashire. Charles Towneley gives us a first-hand account of that last event:

"This occurred one Sunday morning in 1669. The water gushed out near the top of the hill in such quantities, and so suddenly, that it made a breast a yard high, and continued running for about two hours....The houses in the village of Worston, at a distance of two miles from the point of eruption, were so completely inundated, that the furniture in the lower rooms was set afloat by the turbid stream."

Walk across the field to leave by gate. Walk up the green lane to go over stile. Walk up on the right bank of the clough to a marker stone on the moor. A waymarked path leads to the right that lead us over the moor to climb a rake to the ridge above Mearley Clough.

The large cairn commemorates Scouting in Clitheroe since 1907.

Follow the ridge to the stone wind helter. Continue on to a ladder-stile.

Notice the Worston Moor boundary marker built into the wall to the left of the stile. Many such stones are to found on Pendle.

Pass over the stile.

Look down. We are directly above the village of Downham.

A gentle green path leads us over the moor to the Trig. Point summit of Pendle, via ladder-stile.

PENDLE HILL

Love follows not the carefree
leafy path, the smooth and gently
undulating road, a way that
never breaks the rhythm or
the pace, and seeing far
into the distance finds,
no obstacle or danger, no
ambush or surprise.

Instead it cuts a swathe through
thorn and briar, ill shod and
ill prepared it tears the flesh.
It fords the raging torrent and
the crags, are traversed without irons or rope or friend,
and clings with bloodied fingers
whilst oblivion portends.

And I who chose the river and
the rock, above the leafy
path the sheltered glade,
who threshed the summer wheat
and flayed the chaff, yet in damage-
ing the kernel became exiled and
afraid, and turning looking outwards,
sought to lose the inner pain.

As the mighty rain-drop forms
the stream, that joins and drives
the river to its source. So I to
wended through the land unseen,
void of form, diluted,
till I reached an inner shore,
where the debris and the sea-shells
held the answer I have sought.

from LOVE & LONGING
MARK E WARD
LANCASHIRE POET LAUREATE

BIG END, PENDLE TO DOWNHAM

Retrace your footsteps to the wall and walk down to the right to go over wall-stile. Walk directly on and down to Robin Hood's Well.

'Robin Goodfellow, his mad pranks and merry jests,' was published in London in 1639 and was fondly recounted by members of the Pendleside Gentry to cloak their wicked deeds.

Robin is depicted as an ithyphallic god of the witches with young ram's horns sprouting from his forehead, ram's legs, a witches' besom over his left shoulder, a lighted candle in his right hand. Behind him in a ring dance a coven of male and female witches in Puritan costume, a black dog venerates him, a minstrel plays a horn and an owl flies overhead.

It was at this time when the ancient Marian Holy Well on the east flank of Pendle was re-named 'Robin Hood's Well' by the local landowners, partly out of jest, but mainly out of pure hatred of the Roman Catholic Faith that in most quarters of Lancashire still held firm. They doubtlessly remembered too the perjury they had committed against Alice Nutter a Gentlewoman in her eighties, mother of Robert and John Nutter, both Roman Catholic priests who faced martyrdom without fear and with free will.

We Hope and she is always rising, that Mark's beautiful verse will in some way go to restore the harm done to this former Holy Well to the Blessed Virgin and the good name of Pendle – Badon Hill.

> Our Lady of the Fells
> Look down upon your dowry
> Those in hope and trust
> Honest and true to thee shall be

George Fox, a man of God had his great vision at this well that moved him to found the Society of Friend and the Quaker Brethren re-named it to his memory, Fox's Well – good people.

A narrow path skirts the hillside to meet with a wider path that takes us down to the road at Lane Head via three stiles. Go through the gate opposite and down to go over fence stile. Walk up to the left and sit on the bench.

This is the spot where Jessica and her companions rested "near the wall of the pine wood" on the Midsummer Eve so long ago. So shall we rest too and take in the view from the comfort of 'Jessica's Bench.' To the north-west Kemple End and Parlick Pike mark the start of the dramatic and lovely Bowland Fells.

The northern aspect leads up Ribblesdale to the 'Three Peaks' region, Ingleborough and Penyghent stand majestic. To the north-east are the Craven Fells between the Aire and Wharfe.

'Midsummer Night on Pendle,' THREE RIVERS – (the book that started my quest so long ago), by Jessica Lofthouse.

I went through France when
all her corn was cut
and stood in golden sheaves;
I slept in barns, forestalled the dawn
ere swallows left their mellow eves;
oddly or not I even slept
in ditches for God's paupers kept.

John Bradburne, God's Vagabond.

Pass over the wall-stile and walk down the field, over wall-stile and down to go over stiles at Clay House drive.

Clay House and nearby Gerna are fine examples of traditional buildings in the Ribble Valley, recalling the Jacobean period. It is good to see that modern builders are now reviving this good tradition.

Gerna is a solid-looking farmhouse built by William Ashton in 1848. Clay house is of the same period and presents a regal face towards Pendle.

Gerna Farm.

A path now leads us through a recently planted area to pass over a footbridge. Walk directly on by RH fence to go over wall-stile. The path leads us back to Downham via fence-stile and gate.

Wander up to the Post Office Café for a well-earned brew.

DOWNHAM

Nestling under the Lion of Pendle, no intrusive television aerials/dishes, telephone or electricity cables exist here providing a lesson that planning officers should take good heed of.

The information centre, toilets and car park are discreet, blending in well with village surroundings. The working blacksmith's forge by the centre brings life, interest and charm to the visitor and villager alike.

The place-name 'Downham' means 'the estate/manor among hills' and the 'ham' element strongly suggests a Romano-British origin, a type of villa possibly. Near the entrance to the rear of the Hall on the Chatburn road can be found a large rounded stone protruding from the base of the wall. It is known as the Great Stone and is said to mark the grave of two Roman soldiers. The Roman road takes a major turn at Downham and the agger can be clearly traced in the nearby fields.

THE VILLAGE

The church of St. Leonard looks down on the village and the view from the porch is as beautiful as one could behold. A church was established here c.1296, but what we see today is for the most part early 20th century, only the 15th century tower survives from former buildings. This impressive structure holds five bells, three of which are old and two modern. The three old bells may have come from Whalley Abbey and are inscribed thus:

1. 'Vox Augustini sonnet in aure Dei'
2. 'Sta. Margareta ora pro nobis'
3. 'Sta. Katharina ora pro nobis'

(This last bell was recast in 1881 and a new inscription substituted: 'St. Katherine MDCCCLXXXI')

The first two bells have been marked by John Walgrave c.1408.

Opposite the church stands the village inn, once the George and Dragon and now renamed the Assheton Arms. The Assheton coat of arms can be seen above the inn door. It depicts a fool with a scythe – apparently an ancestor feigned madness to escape from enemies – with the motto 'Nea Arrago Nec Dubito.' Across the road and beneath an old sycamore, are the village stocks where wrongdoers were placed in former times.

Down the road and near the beck stands Old Well Hall, the manor house where the manorial steward lived. The Hall is a 16th century pile with low mullioned windows and a projecting two-storey gabled porch. The building is today divided into three cottages.

The manor of Downham was part of the honour of Clitheroe and in 1241 was held in dower of the Countess of Lincoln, widow of John de Lacy. The Dineley family held it from 1354 till 1545, when it was sold to Ralph Greenacres who in turn sold it to Richard Assheton in 1559.

The journal of Nicholas Assheton, a man fond of good sport and drink written in 1617/19, gives one a vivid picture of the life of a country gentlemen in those times: "Eat, drink wine, was merry, and to the field again," sums up his life. Nicholas's heir Ralph, was a Parliamentarian during the Civil War, being placed on the committee for the sequestering of Royalist estates in 1643. A few years later on the 15th August 1648, Oliver Cromwell's men were quartered at Downham on their way to the Battle of Preston. Ralph at this time was a Major-General and in command of all the Roundhead forces of Lancashire.

During this period of the Second Civil War, Ralph had in his command about 1500 foot and 1200 horsemen. His Second-in-Command was Alexander Rigby and in charge of half the cavalry was Nicholas Shuttleworth, son of Richard Shuttleworth of Gawthorpe. After the Battle of Preston, Assheton's men cleared the north-west of Royalist garrisons, recovering possession of both Carlisle and Appleby castles.

The Lancashire Militiamen played a vital role during both Civil Wars for which they were never fully rewarded, paid in short in arrears of monies owed to them. In such personal distress they disbanded, marking the end of an era for Assheton, Rigby and Shuttleworth.

ROOT

Deep, the mountain pine root goes.
Sucking life from dampened stones.
Deep the root it goes.

Out, its children reach,
As laughing waves lick on,
Binding earth around.

Fire, has roamed the mountain side.
The sea now drinks those little stones.
The pines as stick-men stand.

A lament for a wilderness that was once the south-west coast of Crete. Those once wooded heights have been destroyed by the rustic goat-herder trapped in a former age.

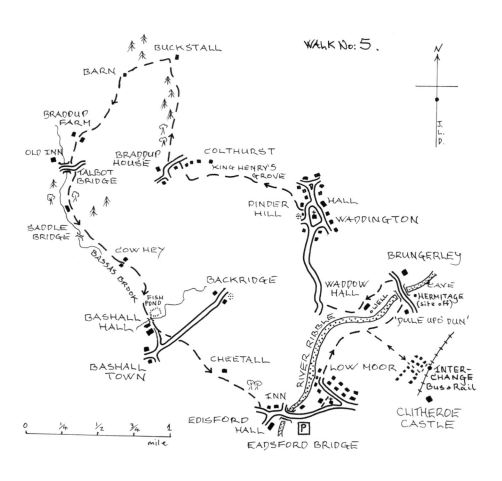

WALK 5

WADDINGTON & BASHALL
A KING ON THE RUN & A KING OF
LEGEND

8 miles easy walking, allow 5½ hours – field paths and pasture

For the casual and regular visitor to Clitheroe this walk is a must, giving one a good taste of the districts surrounding charm and hidden delights.

Waddington and Eadsford Bridge are popular with day trippers, yet secreted close by are enchanting rural aspects preserved from the rude intrusion of the 'Madding Crowd' (discrete caravanning offends very few but filling fields with 'trailer trash' is not the way we should be going).

This walk starts from Eadsford Bridge car park – safe parking. But it can also be started from the INTERCHANGE at Clitheroe by following the directions below (use official car parks in Clitheroe to avoid vandalism).

INTERCHANGE TO RIVERBANK opp' WADDOW HALL

Pass under the railway bridge, left and along by rear of houses to Kirkmoor Road. Right and walk to the bottom of the road to go through kissing-gate at Back Commons. A good path leads to above the river via three kissing-gates.

This field path gives us a good distance view of the Bowland Fells from Parlick Pike to Fair Oak Fell.

EADSFORD BRIDGE CAR PARK TO BRUNGERLEY BRIDGE

Leave the car park and cross the road at crossing to walk past the front of Ribblesdale Pool and over the playing fields to the road at Low Moor Village. Left and around to the right to go along right fork (Ribble Way sign) passing the old Wesleyan School (1866) to pick up a trackway that leads us past the allotments to pass through two kissing-gates at Coe Hill Stables. Follow line of fence to corner...

(The return to Clitheroe)

Walk over to the right to pass through kissing-gate.

This walk back to Clitheroe gives us that classic view of the Castle captured in pen and ink by John Swain.

CLITHEROE CASTLE, FROM NEAR THE RAILWAY STATION.

A good path leads you back to Back Commons via three kissing-gates.

Clitheroe is famous for the good bargains to be had in the many Charity Shops and its Karaoke Pubs.

Friday, Saturday and Sunday nights give way to a 'Frontier, Wild West atmosphere' in the town. Giving great pleasure to young people from the surrounding areas who come to Clitheroe to 'do the rounds' – great, you're only young once.

For those who prefer good talk and good beer without 'boom, boom' music, then Alan is your man at the New Inn (The Inn of Our Lady) on Parson Lane.

...and cross the field to descend a stepped path above the weir.

The frontage of Waddow Hall is now in view.

The riverside path leads us to Brungerley Bridge via kissing-gate and footbridge.

Brungerley Hippings.

BRUNGERLEY BRIDGE

Brungerley Bridge is one of many bridges that before recent boundary changes used to link Lancashire with Yorkshire, as a stone set into the bridge tells us. In the days before the bridge was erected people crossed the Ribble by way of hipping stones set into the bed of the river. These were sited above the modern bridge.

These stones were fraught with danger, due to the narrow channel between rocks forming a deep, slowly circulating whirlpool. Many an unfortunate traveller has met their end whilst traversing the swell. The legend of Peg O'Nell originated here (see below). It was she, it claims, who took the victim to the watery depths of the river.

Local folklore tells us of an old inn that once stood near Brungerley. The inn was known as 'Dule upo' Dun' from its sign representing the Devil galloping madly along upon a dun horse.

Legend holds that a poor tailor of the district sold his soul to Satan in return for riches. However, when finally the moment of his damnation came, the Devil repented and allowed the tailor one more final wish.

The poor tailor seeing a dun horse standing close by wished that his greatest enemy should be carried of to hell upon the stead's back. The Devil granted him his request, mounted the horse and rode furiously away, leaving the tailor to be thankful of his good wits that prevailed over his original greed.

Henry VI would remember Brungerley for quite different reasons. After the Battle of Hexham, the luckless Henry found his way to the Bowland district seeking refuge first at Bolton-by-Bowland and later Waddington. Whilst staying at Waddington Hall he was betrayed and later captured by John Talbot of Salesbury and others in 1464.

They assaulted the Hall, but the deposed king escaped. A little later, whilst crossing the Ribble by the way of Brungerley Hippings, he was overtaken and captured on the Lancashire side of the river, less than a mile north of Clitheroe Castle. He was thence carried bound to a horse to London and imprisoned in the Tower.

Kept in the farmhouse at Brungerley is the figure of a woman carved in oak that once stood in the barn.

Some years ago the barn caught on fire and the farmer bravely rescued the statue from the inferno without regard for himself. A very undaunted and commendable act that we are all in his debt.

Upon examination the figure shows to have been once brightly painted. The design and workmanship are clearly Medieval. Two holes in the back tell one that it was once pegged into a timber beam. The woman is cradling a lamb with her right arm and the style of her clothing is of the 13th and 14th century. Without doubt

SC.

Brungerley Farm
13 – 14th C.

the figure is ecclesiastical in origin, possibly a depiction of St. Agnes. The Emperor Constantine in the 4th century constructed a church around her tomb in Rome, where she was popularly regarded as a protectress of the city.

BRUNGERLEY BRIDGE TO WADDOW HALL

Cross the bridge and follow the road up to enter the grounds of Waddow Hall by stile on left. Follow the drive to the Cattle-grid near the rear of the hall.

Waddow Hall

Seek permission to view front of Hall and 'Peg's Well.'

Was ever a house situated upon a site more beautiful than this? It is transcendently handsome, lying as it does at the foot of a wooded eminence, sheltered on all sides. To the front is a fine inclining lawn, at the foot of which the Ribble flows on its long journey to the Irish Sea.

Local tradition holds that the chieftain Wada, who was put to flight after the Battle of Billington in 798, had his camp on the limestone knolls of Waddow (Wada's Hill) and gave his name to the township of Waddington. (See Walk 3 and Waddington parish church 'History Guide' by Nora Mary Goodchild.)

The house was originally built in Tudor times as a dower house for the Tempest family. In 1267, the name of Roger de Tempest of Bracewell occurs in the Assize Roll as Lord of Waddington. It was he who founded the parish of Waddington and paid a priest to hold service there.

The lands remained in the Tempest Family until 1657, when the last of the male line, Richard Tempest, ruined the estate through his great extravagance. Richard cared more of the life of a dandy than that of a farmer, gambling and drinking his way through the family fortunes. This path was to lead the foolish fellow to the Debtors Prison on whose rat infested floors he was to meet the grim reaper.

The oldest part of the house is enclosed within the present building. This older building is shown in an oil painting of 1690, on a wooden card table. It now hangs in the entrance hall below the main stairs. The Tudor house is now completely hidden behind the Jacobean hall. But the oak-beamed rooms still in use as bedrooms date back to the earlier building.

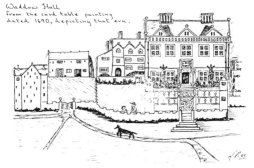

Waddow Hall
from the card table painting
dated 1690, depicting that era.

In the grounds of the Hall is a spring known as Peg O'Nell's Well. By the side of the well there is a headless statue said by some to be a likeness of Peg. Tradition has it that Peg was serving maid at Waddow who fell in love with the eldest son of the family, greatly offending her mistress who expressed a wish that Peg would fall and break her neck. In reply Peg stated that if she did succumb to such a fate she would place a curse upon Waddow – every seventh year the River Ribble would claim a life, though not necessarily a human life. One day Peg slipped on the ice around the well and the malediction was fulfilled. When 'Peg's Night,' the last night of the seventh year, came round, unless an animal was drowned, some human was certain to fall victim of the curse.

Could this stone figure be a statue of St. Helen, Mother of Constantine the Great, once belonging to the church at Waddington before the reformation? (The figure belongs to 1300 to 1400.)

Peg O'Nell's Well
Waddow Hall.

In AD 327at the age of nearly eighty Helen made an energetic and devout pilgrimage to Jerusalem and founded several churches in Palestine, including one in Bethlehem and one on the Mount of Olives.

A tradition which began to crystallize about seventy years after her death holds that she was privileged to discover the Rood of Christ on the Hill of Golgotha.

Certain English chroniclers give currency to the idea that Helen was a daughter of Coel Hen Godebog (Caelius Votepacus), first of the North British Kings after the Roman period; known to many as 'Old King Cole.'

Helen is usually depicted wearing a crown and holding a T-cross and book.

'Hic nascitur Elena regis filia'

The Girl Guide Association purchased Waddow Hall Estate in 1928, and it is now used as a Commonwealth Training Centre. The drawing above shows the Tudor Hall and is featured in the Guild's handbook of Waddow.

The head of the figure is kept inside the Hall.

WADDOW HALL TO THE LOWER BUCK, WADDINGTON

From the cattle-grid follow the footpath on the right around the rear of the hall to go over stile onto trackway. The track leads us to...

The wooded Kemple End of Longridge Fell comes into view with Parlick in the distance.

...the road via gate. Right, to walk on to the road junction below Pinder Hill mound in Waddington.

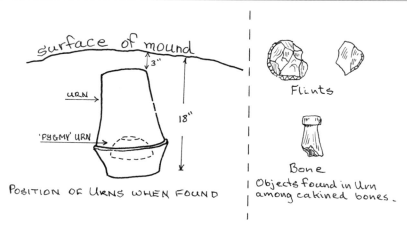

Surface of mound
3"
URN
18"
'PYGMY' URN
POSITION OF URNS WHEN FOUND

Flints

Bone
Objects found in Urn among calcined bones.

PINDER HILL BRONZE AGE BURIAL

To the south-west of the Buck Inn stands a hillock of glacial debris known as Pinder Hill. A small mound on the summit of the rise was excavated in 1887 and yielded a Bronze Age burial urn. Inside the urn, which was inverted, was a mass of broken and partly calcinated bones, more than half filling it.

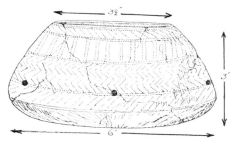

Within this mass was found an 'incense cup/pygmy urn' two worked flints and a worked bone object. The presence of an 'incense cup' is thought by some to mark a female burial, the openwork pattern indicating basketry being particularly the work of women. Yet given the inverted position of the large urn the smaller may have been merely a stopper and may have no other significance.

The flints are the type used for the preparation of skins and preparing throngs of hide. The bone object is a toddle used to fasten a coat or other. These finds are now on display in Clitheroe Castle Museum.

Bronze Age axes have been found at Up-Brooks Farm, Clitheroe and the horn of an 'auroch', extinct during the Bronze Age, in the Ribble at Low Moor.

Buck Inn

Continue on to the Lower Buck.

The Buck Inn, once 'The Roebuck,' is one of the few remaining examples of a true country inn. The landlord, once gamekeeper at Whitewell, serves a good selection of fine ales and beers to be quaffed by an open fire. The food served here is of the finest and very reasonably priced. Good talk and company can be had here without the booming interruption of over amplified juke-box rot, as is the case with so many public houses today.

Waddington's two other pubs, The Sun Inn (now Waddington Arms) and the Buck in th' Vine (now Higher Buck) are good but tend to attract young people and can be somewhat rowdy and the food and drink is only standard fare.

It was in the Lower Buck that I first heard the story of the 'Spectral Sarmatian of Titum' from a rustic raconteur (see Walk 2).

By a wall at the bottom of the inn's cobbled forecourt stands an old horse mounting block, a reminder of a former mode of travel.

ST. HELEN PARISH CHURCH

Such a dedication can often point to a post-Roman British settlement site and a ritual site of the pre-Roman Atecotti peoples of these Isles. Pinder Hill mound is testament to the later.

The Church of St. Helen at Waddington was established by one of my ancestors Roger Tempest in 1267, who also paid for a priest to the run the parish.

St Helen's - Waddington

Of the early foundation only a number of stone heads remain set above an arch below the west window. The tower is the oldest part of the church, being erected in 1501. The octagonal font, with shields carrying the Instruments of he Passion is also of the Perpendicular division of English Gothic architecture. The benches in the former Chapel of St. Oswald now Browsholme Chapel, are Late Stewart and well worth a look at being the most distinctive in the Church. Some Medieval glass forming a composite picture of a figure thought to be Sir Richard Tempest, who rebuilt the church in c.1501 can be found in what is now referred to as the 'Medieval Window.'

Outstanding in the church is The Rood, a glorious example of Austrian wood carving gifted in memory of Francis Parker, vicar from 1894 to 1922.

The Reredos behind the alter is a richly carved depiction of the Nativity. Given the resplendent workmanship, I take this to be of German origin.

A good 'History & Guide,' by Nora Mary Goodchild is available from the church. It covers all aspects of the building with notes on places of interest around Waddington.

WADDINGTON HALL

My drawing depicts the Hall as a ruin in 1815. It was restored by John Waddington, a great romantic and benefactor of the parish church. He described his family as "descendants of Wada Dux, of the divine stock of Woden, who was driven northwards from the Persian Gulf." He is referring here to the year 403, when a vast host of Vandals, Suebi and Alans, escaping from the central European domination of the Huns, crossing the ill-defended Rhine and fanned out across the interior Roman provinces, threatening to invade Britain. In response Britain proclaimed a native Emperor, Canstantine III, who crossed to Gaul and expelled the invaders.

As a ruin in 1815.

As I said Mr Waddington was a romantic, not a historian. Chas Franklin is also of this tradition (see church 'History & Guide') and there is nothing wrong with that – it all adds grist to the mill.

The greater part of the pre-Reformation building is still in existence. The original walls and windows can still be seen in the Great Hall, and the Monk's Room is also of the same early period.

In fact the Monk's Room may be even older; some say that it dates back to the 11th century. The reason for the name is obscure. it has been suggested that the name arose because the room was used by monks travelling between the abbeys of Sawley and Whalley. Others tell of the Black Monk of Abingdon who said to have betrayed Henry VI to the Talbots of Bashall Hall.

Behind the panelling of the Great Hal is the entrance to the 'secret staircase' leading to a spacious room above known as the 'King's Room.' A modern carved cupboard shows pictures of Henry's attempted escape – up the staircase to his bedchamber, down a ladder to the ground and across the fields to Brungerley where he was captured on the Clitheroe side of the river.

The poor fellow's name still lives on in the district, a 'King Henry's Grove' is marked on the OS map. Many years ago there was a small cave in Brungerley Park named 'King Henry's Cave.' This was a former hermits' shelter. The hermit was licensed to celebrate in the chapel of St. Oswald at Waddington Church in 1444. He was William Marshall.

APRIL / MAY 2004

During recent pipe-laying operations, that necessitated boring under the river at Brungerley, a very large cave was discovered on the Clitheroe side of the Ribble below Moorhead School at a point known as 'dangerous corner.' So large was the void that the pipeline had to be diverted for suspension reasons.

Could this be the 'lost' Hermit's Cave, where once King Henry hid?

Also, in the meadow by the bridge known as Segholes – 'hut by the ford,' an artificial platform has been located. Could this be the site of the hermits' shelter for travellers wishing to ford the river at Brungerley in the 15th century?

It is early days yet, but maybe we shall be able to fill in a few more pieces of the local history jigsaw.

In the rear garden of Waddington Hall are two low burial mounds, which are said to date from the 9th century.

WADDINGTON TO BRADDUP HOUSE, COLTHURST

Take the lane behind the Lower Buck and after a few yards turn up the driveway on the right (footpath sign).

The house here is Beechthorpe, once used as a private boarding school. Notice the old waterpump, once used to draw up clean drinking water from an underground spring. The pump now a garden ornament was originally sited opposite Bonny Bar Gate near the Inn.

Pass the house to go through white gate to cross stream and wall stile. Follow path to go over next wall-stile. Bear to the left crossing the field to go over fence-stile.

The fields here are known as 'King Henry's Grove.' He is said to have taken his morning constitution here.

Follow line of the RH hedge, through gateway and across field to go over stile below Hollins Farm. Cross the field to go over stile. Right, then down to the left to go over bridge and through LH gate. Follow fence to go over stile. Follow RH hedge to gated trackway. Here, walk over to your left to go over footbridge. Cross the field directly...

The house up to the right is Colthurst Hall, a lovely house and a lovely aspect. Sir John Holker Attorney General, described as 'a tall, plain, lumbering Lancashire man,' spent his last years at Colthurst till his death in 1882. He was 'by universal consent in the very first rank of his profession.'

...to go over stile by stone wall. Follow lane to the left to go over stile on right. Walk up the field, with the farm on your right and the clump of trees on your left, to go over woodside stile and footbridge to road via gate. Left, and walk down to the corner at Braddup House.

Braddup House. A.D. 1669

BRADDUP HOUSE

BRADDUP HOUSE

Here we have a fine old farmhouse of the late-Stewart period. I like the innovation from that time of the long stairwell window. The datestone at the rear is of 1669, R. E. W. with another to be viewed on the front of the building.

We now go up Whinney Lane a lovely wooded strip, once part of the old Browsholme Road. Today it provides a natural habitat for many types of wildlife and flora – a nature lovers paradise.

BRADDUP HOUSE TO TALBOT BRIDGE

Pass through the field gate on the right of the house rear and enter wood via gate. Follow brideway up through the wood to farm lane via gate. Right, through gates to go left, up by the edge of the wood, over stiles to go through field gate. Pass through next gate and follow LH fence/wall to meet with farm track via gates. Go through gate on left and follow RH fence to the ruin of Burbles Hill Barn via three gates.

We have now gained a good view of Pendle and Longridge Fell.

From the back (west face) of the barn cross the field on a left-diagonal to end of far hedgerow to cross stream and stile. Cross this field on the same left-diagonal to go over stile by gate. Follow RH fence to enter Braddup Farm via stile and gate.

What a delightful rustic setting – very pleasing.

Pass through farmyard to front of house. A few yards down the lane we go over a ladder-stile. Follow overhead cables to brook and Talbot Bridge via gate.

TALBOT BRIDGE

The 17th century bridge straddles Bashall Brook carrying 'Rabbit Lane,' an old trade route through the district. Notice the carved stones built into the parapet informing us why and when the bridge was built.

The house standing near the bridge was once the Woolpack Inn, giving a clue to the traveller's trade in bygone days.

When looking at old routes that used draw horses, you will find an inn, or building that was once such, about every two miles. Draw horses need to take in more water than you would think.

TALBOT BRIDGE TO BASHALL HALL

On coming out on to the road, walk up to the left for 40 yards to leave by stile on right at end of wood. Follow RH fence down to go through field gate. Follow line of new plantation...

I remember when Mr. Backhouse planted these trees. Now all is maturing well he deserves full credit for the wide variety displayed here – a good example to others.

...down to go over stile by new farm building, walk on and follow track to the left to go over stile by gate to Saddle Bridge.

Upon finding Saddle Bridge the eyes are greeted by a veritable fairyland. What tales could people tell of the folk who have oft crossed this enchanted bridge. Nestling in an idyllic setting and bridge rises like a huge stone saddle over the water.

Saddle Bridge.

It is said that kind fairies erected the bridge in a single night, having taken pity on an aged woodcutter who was being sorely tormented by a witch who lived near another crossing further upstream.

Follow Bashall Brook down to go over fence-stile. Follow line of fence to enter Cow Hey housing enclave. Follow the lane down to the bridge at Bashall Hall.

BASHALL HALL

Bashall Hall was built by the Talbot family and is an uncommonly curious and

Bashall Hall

impressive house. Constructed over many periods, Early Georgian and Elizabethan stand side by side.

The whole is surrounded by walled gardens and accessory buildings. One of these buildings, an Early Georgian Summer House with large vases on top, brings a touch of Versailles to Bashall.

The drawing pictures the old barracks of the Talbots' retinue of troops. Much half-timbered work still remains, and on the other side a wooden gallery runs the length of the first floor. Looking up one almost expects to see a trooper polishing up his boots or putting a shine upon his breast-plate, so good is the restoration work.

It was from this Hall that John Talbot of Salesbury, his cousin Thomas Talbot, son and heir to Sir Edmund Talbot of Bashall, and James Harrington set out to effect the capture of King Henry VI, who was in hiding at Waddington Hall.

In the tumult of the Wars of the Roses many local families were torn as to where their loyalties lay – should they support the deposed Henry VI or the new king, Edward IV?

Feeling that the tide had turned in his favour, Henry and his army crossed the border from Scotland into England, but they were defeated at the Battles of Hegeley Moor and Hexham.

Fleeing for his life Henry rode south and sought refuge for some time at Bolton Hall in Bowland, home of Sir Ralph Pudsay. This poor man, subject to fits of madness, could not remain from the authorities notice long, and soon circumstances forced him to leave Sir Ralph's home and flee to Waddington Hall, which at that time was the occasional residence of Sir John Tempest of Bracewell.

Sir John was married to a Talbot, and soon news of the arrival of the Lancastrian King came to the ears of Thomas Talbot of Bashall. The Talbots eager to gain favour with King Edward, rode out in force and surrounded the Hall where the King was at dinner.

Upon hearing the house was beset, Henry contrived to escape, and fled towards the river, hoping to put that between himself and his enemies. His pursuers however, were too many and too eager for him. He was captured, after crossing the hipping stones, in a wood close by. From here he was conducted to London in the most ignominious manner, with his legs fastened to the stirrups of the sorry nag on which he was mounted, and an insulting placard fixed to his shoulders.

On July 9th 1465, the Talbots were granted a reward for this service. Even today some see the Talbots' action as an act of treachery, but given those troubled times who is to say what was right or wrong?

BASHALL HALL TO EADSFORD BRIDGE

From the bridge, walk up the drive to leave by a double field gate on the left. Walk up the hill to pass over stile to the left of the tall sycamore tree, onto Twitter Lane to go over stile opposite.

THE BATTLE OF BASSAS BROOK

The area we now look upon, in the 'Crook o' Bassas Brook,' is known as

Backridge and here is said to have been fought an ancient battle between Sarmatian Cavalry, led by Arthur and Anglo-Saxon invaders from Europe.

In Whitaker's 'History of Whalley' is a mention of age-old battlefield at Backridge:

"In a line betwixt Waddington and Bashall, but especially about Backridge, have been discovered of late (early 1800's), in digging for gravel, many skeletons, which from the manner in which they lay, must indicate the place of some great engagement.

From the situation of the place, I was first inclined to refer these appearances to the battle fought on Clitheroe Moor, between David the First of Scotland and the forces of King Stephen, as part of the line, though north of the Ribble, is scarcely more than half a mile from that place.

But in digging gravel for the highways near Backridge, among some of these Skeletons, was found a broken celt (battle axe), which was brought to me and I am assured that some brass fibulae (cloak fastener) were discovered about the same time and place.

The inference to be drawn from this last circumstance is, that on this spot has been a great engagement between the Romans and Britons." From Addenda to the edition of 1818.

Local tradition tells of the 'Battle of Bassas Brook,' where King Arthur and his forces defeated the Saxons under Tarquin forcing them back over the Pennines to York.

Within this ancient British land,
In Lancashire I understand,
Near Manchester there lived a knight of fame,
Of a prodigious strength and might,
Who vanquished many worthy knights;
A giant great, and Tarquin was his name.

Ballad of Sir Tarquin

The ballad goes on to tell us that Tarquin devoured a child daily at his morning repast.

In the final part of the ballad Tarquin is overthrown by Sir Lancelot of the Lake (Martin Mere), who ruled over the western part of Lancashire (then Valentia).

A document in Nennius, a collection of historical records first put together in the 8th century, list twelve of Arthur's battles:

The Battle of –

1)	the river Glen	2-5)	the river Douglas
6)	the river Bassas	7)	Celidon Forest
8)	Fort Guinnion	9)	the City of the Legion
10)	the river Tribruit	11)	Agned Hill, or Bregion
12)	Badon Hill (Pendle)		(Brougham in Westmoreland)

Nennius also writes that "Arthur bore the image of the Blessed Virgin on his shield" during these battles with the Saxons.

(Historia Brittonum, chap. 56.)

For a full account of Arthur the Sarmatian read:
'FROM VALENTIA TO RHEGED – The Origins of Lancashire'
Dr. P. G. Dixon, Aussteiger Publications.
ISBN 1 872764 12 6 , 2005.

Other suppose it to be the site of the Battle of Brunanburh fought near a hill called Weondun, where there had been a pagan temple, in A.D. 937. At the hill fort of Brunanburh Athelstan defeated a Norse-British confederacy led by Anlaf of Dublin and Constantine, King of the Scots. The site has never been identified and it may well be sited within Blackburnshire. Whatever the case Backridge holds its secrets well.

Walk down to go over stile by gate. Cross the field on a slight right diagonal to go over ditch and over footbridge and stile in hedge. Walk up to go over fence-stile onto Cheetall Farm lane.

Pass over stile opposite and walk on to go over corner fence-stile. Follow LH fence to end of small wood, then head for RH corner of field to go over stile into road. Left, walk down to the junction.

Edisford Hall is the farm on the right. To the left is Eadsford Bridge Inn and Eadsford Bridge, just below the car park.

EDISFORD HALL

Edisford Hall.

Edisford Hall stands upon the site of the Leper Hospital of Saint Nicholas. The hospital was founded by the burgesses of Clitheroe some time after 1140. The first charter of this hospital, undated, is one in which John, son of Ralph de Clitheroe granted three acres of land in Sidhill (Siddows) to the lepers in Edisford.

Another early charter, by Orme de Hammerton, granted "to God, St Nicholas of the house of Edisford and to the brother lepers of the same dwelling with Reginald (warden) two acres on Schetill (Cheetall)." In 1211, Roger de Lacy, Constable of Chester, bequeathed to the hospital four acres of land in Baldwin Hill.

In c.1317, when Richard de Edisforth was warden, the house contained no lepers (the affliction of those poor men is now thought to have been elephantitis brought back from the Crusades in the East and not that of leprosy). Eventually, in 1351, the house having no staff or 'lepers,' Hugh de Clitheroe, the bailiff, requested that the Abbot and Convent at Whalley take possession of the hospital and its lands.

The final notice of the hospital is in 1508 when John Paslew, the last abbot of Whalley, and the burgesses of Clitheroe jointly presented Sir William Heard to the Chapel of St. Nicholas of Edisford, which was vacant as a result of the death of the previous holder of the office, Sir John Dineley.

Still to be made out in stonework at the rear of the farmhouse are a number of shields set in Perpendicular arches bearing arms. In particular, note the lion rampant and fret of Roger de Lacy.

Opposite the cobbled entrance to Edisford Hall Houses (these sets were laid by Andrew Backhouse and myself in 1999, on a dry base mix 2ft. in depth, you can run a tank over them, so well are they laid), behind the hedge in Thirty Acres field is the ancient well of the former Hospital, now a cattle watering-place. The well was rich in Germanium, known for its healing properties.

Thirty Acres Farm has a datestone of 1591 in the porch, one of the oldest buildings in the area.

EADSFORD BRIDGE

The bridge is a medieval stone structure and the original ribwork can still be seen under the central arch. In the 1300s tolls were taken for portage (carriage of goods across the bridge) from traders using the Lancaster-Clitheroe medieval way. The bridge was also the site of a battle some 870 years ago.

In 1138 King David of Scotland led his army on a raid into England. He detached part of his army into Yorkshire under his nephew, William Fitz Duncan. With great carnage they laid waste the monastery of Furness and the province of Craven with fire and sword.

On the 10th June that year William was attacked by the forces of King Stephen at Eadsford Bridge. William routed this force and much blood was split by his men, forever staining the fields of Edisford with the quartered bodies of the King's men. This raid also penetrated into Coupland where Calder Abbey was plundered and its inhabitants put to the sword.

Old charters tell as that William Fitz Duncan had already acquired the district north of the Ribble at Edisford along with Skipton in Craven by his marriage to Alice, one of the co-heiresses of William Meschin, the brother of Rannulf Earl of Chester.

This being the case it seems likely that he made the attack because he was being forcibly kept out of his inheritance. Or perhaps he had a private feud with his neighbour, Ilbert de Lacy, lord of the honour of Clitheroe, who also held lands in Craven.

The battlefield has now given way to more pleasant pursuits. an indoor swimming pool, pitch and put course, children's playground, an excellent caravan and camping site and a miniature railway all provide a splendid amenity for visitors to the district. The riverside path down to Siddows provides exercise for the motorists' legs.

The hotel across the river is the Edisford Bridge Hotel and provides bar snacks and evening suppers. The pub sign depicts the sturdy bridge, and the seats below permit the weary traveller to rest his legs.

"These peoples (Sarmatians), whose habits are more suited to brigandage than to open warfare, use long spears and breastplates made of polished horn attached like scales to a linen backing... They cover enormous distances either in pursuit or flight, riding horses that are swift and tractable."

Ammianus Marcellinus, AD 358.

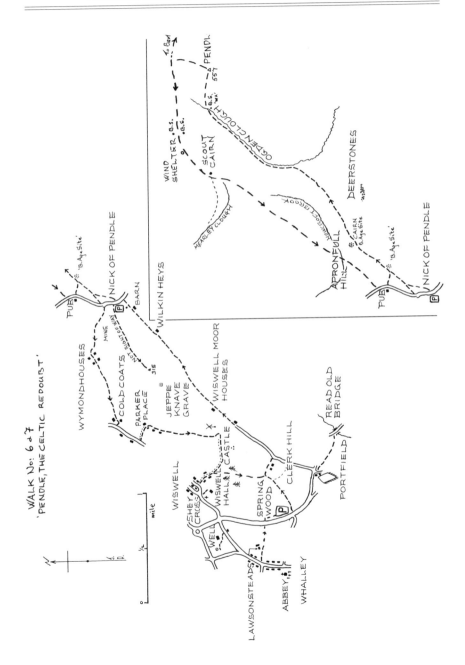

WALKS 6 & 7

WHALLEY, NICK OF PENDLE, PENDLE, WYMONDHOUSES & WISWELL

'PENDLE, THE CELTIC REDOUBT'

7 & 7 miles, 3 hours or 14 miles, 6 hours – moorland and field, easy walking.

LUNCH: Wellsprings, Nick of Pendle or Freemasons Arms, Wiswell.

START: Whalley or Spring Wood above Whalley, or Nick of Pendle.

Whalley is a good start for those who have come by train or bus. Car users will find parking in Whalley difficult, so I suggest Spring Wood car park – very safe with toilets. Parking is also available at Wellsprings, Nick of Pendle – toilets in pub.

MAPS: Explorer ™ OL 41 & OL 287

I describe both walks together as one figure of eight, the crossing point being the Nick of Pendle.

This walk takes us from above the Whalley gorge and along the spine of Pendle to the summit cairn. In the early days of our history this hill gave shelter and life to farmers and workers in stone and bronze, who later moved from their hilltop redoubt to clear and settle the valley floors.

Signs of that early time are to be seen in the number of mounds and ringbanked cairns scattered over the higher ground, Jeppe Knave Grave denuded tumulus and Devil's Apronfull ring-banked cairn to name but two.

Finds of man's early tools have been few; as is only to be expected, time and the build up of peat tend to put all things out of reach.

WHALLEY TO SPRING WOOD

Thanks to Emma Murray at Clitheroe TIC we do not have to cross the A671 'death trap' road. She very kindly pointed out to me an 'underground' way that I never knew about. Thank you Emma, John.

From the Bus Station, turn right and walk up to the mini-roundabout to go up Brooks Lane.

When you come to the brick built villas, notice the climber Multijunga (Wisteria floribunda) on the central dwelling. This is by far my favourite perfumed climber, its long recemes are lovely when left to hang.

Upon reaching the footpath-post...

Manor House and Lawsonsteads are on the right. Manor House was once the home of the Brooks family, early Lancashire bankers and developers, Whalley Range in Manchester was built by one of the family. The house dates from the 16th century and inside can be found a massive inglenook fireplace with a beehive bread oven.

Built into the barn at Lawsonsteads are a number of decorated fragments of stonework from Whalley Abbey.

...take the RH track via gate, to pass over a stile. Walk up by the wood to go over stile on left into wood.

In Spring wild garlic, bluebells and the purple herb Robert carpet the woodland floor. In Summer honeysuckle and enchanter's nightshade hold forth.

A good path leads us through the wood and under the motorway into Spring Wood via kissing gate. Walk to the right to the car park, toilets and refreshments.

SPRING WOOD CAR PARK TO CLERK HILL

Come out of the car park and walk to the left to pass over stile onto golf course. Follow left-hand fence up to pass over footbridge on left. Walk up the field diagonally to follow fence up to go over stile and walk up to pass over two stiles. Follow the wall around the rear of Clerk Hill to the driveway. Walk along the driveway to the road (the grounds of Clerk Hill are private).

We are now at the rear of Clerk Hill House. Notice the Coach House on the right. The keystone of the double arch bears a date of 1772 with the initials J. W. above. With the cobbled floor and little fireplace, nothing has changed since it was built.

CLERK HILL

In the 13th century Clerk Hill was named Snelleshowe meaning 'the hill of Sniallr'. Sniallr or Snell would have been numbered among those Hiberno-Norse that erected the crosses in the churchyard at Whalley, if that place was the original siting. The charming Georgian mansion that stands at Clerk Hill today was built by the Whalley family between 1715 and 1772.

To the north-east of Clerk Hill stands Castle Wood, in which can be found the ruins of a once castellated folly known as Baby House Towers. Sadly this was demolished during the 1940s by men of the Royal Engineers under the instruction of a local farmer, annoyed by people visiting the site.

Down the road from Clerk Hill stands the hillfort of Portfield. Permission to view the earthworks must first be sought from the owners of Portfield House.

PORTFIELD HILLFORT

Portfield is the birthplace of my lifelong friend, John Mitchell, with whom I spent my youth exploring all things of an ancient nature. Incredibly, his home was the most ancient of them.

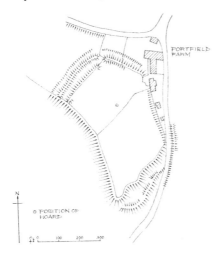

The farmstead stands on the site of Portfield Hall, home of the Braddyll family whose original seat was the House of Braddyll with Brockhall on the banks of the Ribble. When the Hall was demolished the stones were used to build the Whalley Arms Inn. An old window from the Hall can be seen in the gable of he Inn, and with it a date 1781 and the initials R. C.

The Great Barn of Portfield was erected by the monks of Whalley Abbey as a tithe barn; a tithe was a tenth part of agricultural produce paid as a tax. The timber construction within is the finest surviving example of early 14th century workmanship in the entire area.

Until recent times, Portfield was thought to be the site of a Roman camp or signal station. However, the findings of the summer of 1966 during pipe-laying operations across the site, changed the thinking on the early history of Lancashire.

The camp lies on the slight southward-facing promontory. Clear traces of defensive works exist on the north-west. These consist of a bivallate bank and ditch structure. Further defences probably existed on the east and south-east. But no traces survive.

The 1960s excavation revealed two phases of construction. The earliest consisted of a single, stone-revetted rampart without a ditch situated some 20ft. Behind the present inner rampart. The first rampart was subsequently levelled and the existing inner rampart constructed. This was again revetted in stone on its inner and outer faces having a clay core. It was separated from its ditch by a berm 20ft. wide. The outer bank and ditch may originally have had a slight conterscarp bank.

This early investigation redefined the camp as an Iron Age hill fort. The discovery of a Bronze Age hoard deposited in the 7th century B. C., revealed in the 1966 pipe laying operations, lends support to the idea that many of the hilltops later fortified in the Iron Age, as is the case at Portfield, may have originated as settlements even as early as 2000 B.C.

Portfield Camp is one of five hillforts, all in North Lancashire. With the exception of a large camp at Warton Crag the forts are all small in comparison with the great fortified earthworks of the South and reflect the broken nature of the countryside and a smaller more scattered population. The siting of the hoard near the junction of the river Calder with the Ribble points to a still active trade link along a trans-Pennine route of long standing.

THE PORTFIELD HOARD

1. Bronze, single-looped, socketed axe, sub-rectangular at mouth, with quadrangular body and expanded curved cutting-edge. Heavy moulding at the mouth with lighter moulding beneath from which descend three vertical, parallel ribs. Two vertical mouldings inside the socket.

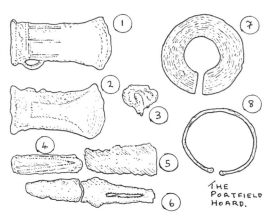

THE PORTFIELD HOARD.

2. Bronze, single-looped, socketed axe, oval at mouth, with octagonal faceted body and expanded curved cutting edge. Deep but slight moulding at the mouth.

3. Piece of rough bronze resembling a splash with bent-over runner.

4. Lower half of a bronze socketed gouge, lacking mouth and cutting-edge.

5. Part of a bronze socketed gouge, lacking mouth and bevelled edge.

6. Two pieces forming a tanged knife with central rib on each side of tang. The lower part of the blade is missing and much of the bronze cutting edges are corroded.

7. Gold penannular tress-ring of hollow triangular section, decorated with fine concentric incised lines made with a tracer. The ring is an Irish import and shows the maintenance of Hibernian contact at this period.

8. Gold plain penannular bracelet of flattened, slightly hollow D-section with externally expanded terminals. This is a 7th century B.C. copy in gold of the variant type of Covesea bronze bracelet. The gold is Irish but this type of bracelet is unknown in Ireland and therefore must have been made in or for the British northern market.

A flint arrowhead was found on the site in 1974, and is dated c.750 B.C.

Replicas of the hoard can be seen in both Ribchester and Blackburn Museums. The small fragment of rough metal (no. 3), clearly a by-product of smelting, shows that the hoard was the property of an actual bronze-smith. Recent excavations on the site have produced finds of Mesolithic flints, Neolithic Grimston ware and Beaker pottery as well as Late Bronze Age/Early Iron Age and Romano/British finds all pointing to the importance of the hill at Portfield through prehistoric times.

CLERK HILL TO NICK OF PENDLE

Follow the road up to Wiswell Moor Houses, then follow the well-defined trackway to pass the rear of Wilkin Heys and on, passing Parsley or Paslew Barn to the Sabden Road. Walk up to the Nick.

A path leads south-west along the ridge to the Trig. Pt. summit of Wiswell Moor. Beyond this the land falls and in the hollow there are a group of stones known as 'Jeppe Knave Grave.' The site belongs to Parker Place Farm and permission is required to visit the site.

JEPPE KNAVE GRAVE

To the west of Wilkin Heys, just below the triangulation point, is a small depression in the moorland turf containing rocks and stones of various sizes. Upon the largest stone are inscribed the words 'JEPPE KNAVE GRAVE' and a cross. The stone is said to mark the final resting place of Jeppe Curteys, a local robber who was decapitated for his crimes in the first year of Edward III, 1327.

In those times the punishment of decapitation was usual, being reserved for those of noble birth. The full story of Jeppe's crimes and trail would no doubt making an intriguing one indeed.

The grave spot itself is now thought to mark the site of a Bronze Age denuded tumulus, being a circular feature of around 20ft. in diameter. The outer ring of stones can be discerned in the rough pasture at the perimeter – yellow in dry conditions, showing the circular shape.

A mile north-west of the site is Carriers Croft where in 1968 another circular feature was discovered. During the excavation between 1968 and 1975, three collared urns along with a gold cylinder and a bone toddle were found. These are now on display in Clitheroe Castle Museum.

THE DEVIL'S APRONFULL

This ring of stones stands upon the highest point of Pendleton Moor by the pathway that leads from Nick of Pendle to the summit. The site is now recognised as a Bronze Age ring bank cairn, a paved outer ring with a central cairn of loose stones. Due to natural erosion and the absence of the build up of peat, this feature can clearly be discerned at ground level, all that remains of a once communal living hut over 3,000 years old. The outer ring is all the remains of the stone outer wall, the inner cairn the central heath, all roofed by timbers covered in turf in much the same way as the old Highland crofts.

Urn burials beneath the floor level are very common in these structures, only an excavation would establish the case here. A worthwhile task for some local archaeology group.

THE NICK OF PENDLE TO PENDLE SUMMIT

A broad track leaves the road near to the car park and leads us on past Apronfull Hill up and over Black Hill into the upper reaches of Ogden Clough. We now follow the clough up to meet with a paved path that leads us up and over Barley Moor to the summit Pendle.

PENDLE HILL

The lion head of Pendle, with its tail resting in Pleasington and its fore paws gripping Barnoldswick, stands sentinel at the eastern portal to Lancashire. Inspiration to some and a curse to others, friendly and welcoming on a fine clear day, menacing and towering on those darker rainswept days, but always Pendle in all her moods. Legend, myth and fact have conspired to impress this hill deep into the Northern psyche, providing a Folk with an immortal image of these northlands.

The summit, 557m. above sea level (1827 ft.), is marked by a triangulation point that stands on the site of an old fire-beacon, which it turn is said to have been built upon an ancient burial mound.

Fire-beacons sited upon prominent hills are not uncommon in Lancashire and provide a quick way of spreading news of national or regional emergencies. The Pendle beacon has been used since Roman times up to present day.

It was from this summit in 1652, that George Fox had his great vision that moved him to found the Quakers, or Society of Friends, one of the earliest meeting places being sited at Twiston.

Towneley Hall Museum hold the major archaeological finds from the Forest side of Pendle, these include: a perforated stone mallet found at Newchurch, a gritstone axe-hammer with a polished surface found in Ogden Clough, a jadeite polished stone axe/adze and a Late Bronze Age socketed axe, both found on Pendle.

The view from the heights are magnificent – the Lakes, Bowland Fells, Ingleborough, Pen-y-Ghent, Malham Scars, the Aire Gap and the Pennine backbone all seem to gather round this most well known and loved of Lancashire's hills.

PENDLE SUMMIT TO WELL SPRINGS INN.

From the Trig. Pt. walk in a NNE towards a wall to go over ladder stile.

Follow a green track across the moor to pass over wall-stile (notice boundary stone built into wall on left marked with a 'D' – Downham, a bench mark). Follow a cairned path along the edge of the escarpment, past the stone wind shelter and on to the tall, well-built Scout Cairn.

From Scout Cairn head over to the left to skirt the head of

Mearley Clough and pick up a path that heads south-west across rough moorland to reach a broken wall. Pass over and continue on alongside the wall on the right and on to the head of ridge. Follow the path down the steep descent to cross the stream by the iron post. Follow the clear path on, then across the slightly rising moor to head over to the left to join the road. Walk up the road to the Well Springs Inn.

WELL SPRINGS INN TO WYMONDHOUSES

Walk up the road to pass over stile by gate on right and walk down the track to pass over next stile by gate. Follow old trackway down to Wymondhouses.

Just beyond the old trackway is a small lead mine, once worked by the lay brothers of Whalley Abbey. It is still possible to find bits of lead today.

Did you notice the large stone on the right, just beyond Paslew Barn as you came up to the Nick road earlier? No, you missed it, but there is always next time. This standing stone is known as the 'Coffin Stone.' It was used to rest coffins en route from the Forest of Pendle to Whalley before the Newchurch was built in Goldshaw Booth.

WYMONDHOUSES

Wymondhouses is first recorded in 1285 as Wymotehuses, meaning 'Wigmund's House.' By the 14th century it had the status of a small hamlet. The farmstead we see today belongs to the 17th century, the sole survivor of the once tiny village.

WYMONDHOUSES

Above the front door of the house is a tablet with the following inscribed upon it: Thomas Jollie Founded the First Congregational Church Here in 1667. Here in those days of religious persecution and the Five Mile Act, the Rev. Thomas Jollie, once minister at Altham until he was expelled in 1662, held services for those who broke away from the church and followed him.

In those days the barn served as a chapel (dated 1669 with the initials T. I. being those of Thomas Jollie); today the Jollie Memorial Chapel is sited at Barrow. Services were held in secret in the barn until the Act of Toleration in 1689, when the house was granted a licence for services. By all accounts Jollie was a hard man well known for his fire and brimstone speeches and sermons.

Standing in the garden of the mullioned fronted farmhouse is a fragment of an inscribed stone tablet bearing the remains of some Biblical quotation. The tablet was originally set above the doorway of one of the now demolished houses at Wymondhouses.

WYMONDHOUSES TO COLD COATS

Enter farmyard and pass through the gate facing you by the cattle shed and walk directly on to cross Audley Clough via stile up into field. Cross the field on a right diagonal to go over stile by gate and walk on to enter Cold Coats via gate.

COLD COATS

Cold Coats, part of Great Mytton parish, contains one farmstead that itself contains many interesting features. Built into the gable end is a window from the Abbey at Whalley and the walls of the building contain many decorated fragments of masonry from the same source and a shield bearing the initials T. W. A. (Thomas and Alice Walmsley).

COLD COATS TO WISWELL

Walk down the farm lane to the road, left and walk on to go up Parker Place Farm drive to go through small gate at rear of house. Walk to the right to pass through gateway and on to enter Wiswell Eaves.

Wiswell Eaves is a substantial 17th century building. Notice the ogee-head three-light window in the east gable and many standard mullioned windows.

I am informed that there was once a mill at Wiswell Eaves, but know little else.

Walk on to go through two gates, then take the track up the hillside to enter field via gate. Continue on, and then walk up to far top corner of field to go over wall-stile set in corner. Walk up to meet a trackway by the wood. This track leads us down to Wiswell via 3 gates.

WISWELL

The village of Wiswell grew up around an old spring, known in the 12th century as Wisa's Well or as some would have The Wise Woman's Well, in the southern corner of the ancient Reeves manor of Pendleton.

By the bank of the brook, below Wiswell Hall farm, stands Wiswell Shey Cross. This restored cross in an ancient socket is also known as the Weeping Cross. It marks the place of halt for funeral processions en route for Whalley churchyard from the outlaying districts below Pendle and Clitheroe.

Wiswell Hall farm stands close to the site of the demolished Wiswell Hall. The drawing shows the Hall in 1669, home then of Thurstan Tomlinson whose datestone is now built into one of the farm outbuildings. A window from the old Hall is now built into the farmhouse.

WISWELL HALL

The former Hall was the birthplace of the last Abbott of Whalley Abbey, the fiery John Paslew. In 1536 Paslew and the Whaley Monks were implied to have been involved in the protest against the suppression of the lesser monastic houses, known to history as 'Pilgrimage of Grace'.

The ill-conceived venture collapsed in October of that year. Abbott Paslew, some Whalley Monks, along with the Abbott of Sawley Thomas Bolton and some of his monks were tried for treason and condemned to death.

WISWELL HALL

Wiswell Hall

Paslew with the Whalley Monk named Haydock together with the Sawley monk Richard Eastgate were hung, drawn and quartered at Lancaster. The remains of Paslew's body were brought back to Whalley to be displayed on the local gibbet at Little Imps Field.

The Abbey was seized by the crown, and later sold in 1553, to Richard Assheton and John Braddyll, both engaged in the suppression of the rebellion.

Within the older Wiswell Hall was Paslew's private chapel. The font from which can be found at the rear of the nave of Whalley church. The holy water stoop from the chapel is used today as a baptismal font in Immanuel Church, Feniscowls near Blackburn.

A carved figure in stone of Abbott Paslew in prayer is built in above a window in one of the roadside cottages.

Vicarage House, the first one notices on entering the village from Whalley, is a good example of local architecture and contains within its fabric an older 16th Century dwelling. During the 17th Century the house belonged to Crombrocks (Crombleholme) family of Catholic yeoman stock.

During those dark times the house, given its secluded position, became a place for secret worship and a number of hiding holes can be found in the house. The family remained Catholics until Dorothea Crombocks, the last of the family line, turned Protestant when she married the vicar of Whalley in

1665, hence the houses present name, 'The Old Vicarage'.

HIGH WALL WELL

High Wall Well is sited inside the grounds of the former Bramley Mead Hospital. Covered by a grotto-type structure, the waters are reached by descending three steps. It is said to be the clearest and purest spring in Whalley district, the only one that was never polluted.

Perhaps for this reason the Abbey monks laid leaden pipes from the well into their convent, sections of which have been located by the local History and Archaeological Society.

WISWELL TO CLERK HILL/SPRING WOOD

Walk back up Moor Lane, through gate, and then over stile by the gate on right. Follow path to enter pine wood via stile.

Amid these tall pines I get a real sense of repose: the colouration of the bark is alive and overflowing, and the lofty, slender trunks are Nature's Cathedral piers.

The woods are lovely, dark and deep,
But I have promises to keep,
And miles to go before I sleep,
And miles to go before I sleep.

Robert Frost.

Upon leaving the wood, walk directly on (via two stiles) to a seat below a ruinous barn.

Sit a while and look down upon Whalley.

PLEASINGTON PRIORY

There once a great Abbey stood, upon the site of a former Celtic Monastery, its pinnacles reaching the then sky in praise of the Blessed Virgin Mary. Only the outline and a few fragments of the church remain. But at Pleasington Priory, The Church of St. Mary and John the Baptist, one can see what the frontage of the church would have looked like.

The former Monastery of Paegnalaech (Whalley) was founded by Arthur the Sarmatian and dedicated to the Blessed Virgin, whose image he bore upon his shield. The Sarmatians had a large veteran settlement centred upon Whalley, that later became known as Blackburnshire (with Bowland). Whalley is the Camelot of legend and Pandle Hill was Mount Badon.

First mention of Whalley can be found in Bede and the Anglo-Saxon Chronicle for the year 664. During that year Bishop Tuda visited these areas west of the Pennines to oversee the submission of the Celtic Church to Roman rites. While at Whalley, he died from the outbreak of the Bubonic Plague recorded for that year, a horrific slayer that was given its momentum by the Synod of Whitby. Bishop Tuda was buried at Whalley and three High Crosses erected in his memory.

Clearly Whalley was considered a significant and important site in those times.

The three stiles below the seat lead us back down the edge of the golf course to Spring Wood picnic area.

Spokes of a wheel, Lao Tzu
Tobacco whisked away
Rain makes water flow
Spokes of a wheel, Lao Tzu
Up on a mountain
Upanishads
Chicken soup and rice
Down at the well
Move over the sky
Walk a long way
Goodbye, Lao Tzu
       John
(In memory of Jaana)

THE WHALLEY CHURCHYARD CROSSES

NORTH CHANCEL WALL, WHALLEY

THE PRIEST'S DOOR
WHALLEY

Roman
Altar,
Whalley
Church.